To Jill, Mark and Jim who have taught me so much about divorce.

To Paul who's made the journey with me.

To Fran and Sue, many thanks!

~ BgF

Six-Word Lessons on Surviving Divorce

Six-Word Lessons on
SURVIVING
DIVORCE
100 Lessons to Help You Cope and Reach a New Normal

Barbara G. Feinberg, LSIW-S, IMFT

Published by Pacelli Publishing
Bellevue, Washington

Six-Word Lessons on Surviving Divorce

All rights reserved. No part of this book may be reproduced or transmitted in any form or by any means, electronic or mechanical including photocopying, recording or by any information storage or retrieval system, without the written permission of the publisher, except where permitted by law.

Limit of Liability: While the author and the publisher have used their best efforts in preparing this book, they make no representation or warranties with respect to accuracy or completeness of the content of this book. The advice and strategies contained herein may not be suitable for your situation. Consult with a professional when appropriate.

Copyright © 2012 by Barbara G. Feinberg

Cover and interior design by Pacelli Publishing

Published by Pacelli Publishing
9905 Lake Washington Blvd. NE, #D-103
Bellevue, Washington 98004

ISBN-10: 1-933750-30-8
ISBN-13: 978-1-933750-30-9

The decision, process and aftermath associated with ending a committed relationship are enormously complex, disruptive and highly emotional. This process can affect the couple, their children, and everyone they know.

In this *Six Word Lessons* book, you'll find 100 short, practical tips and ideas to help you deal with divorce. This brief overview provides a quick look at the many issues facing those considering or ending a committed relationship, and after a divorce.

Three circumstances that I've not addressed explicitly:

1. While this book is oriented around marriages *per se,* many chapters apply to ending committed relationships not formalized in the eyes of the law.

2. I discuss the challenges associated with deciding to end a marriage. I recognize that in many instances one partner has made that decision, while the other can only comply. However, the balance of the book can be useful nonetheless.

3. Many couples ending a committed relationship don't have children.

I hope this material will give you a starting place as you think about this critical decision, and will help you as you move forward or stay where you are.

Let me know what you think at futurescoach.net.

~ Barbara G. Feinberg, LISW-S, IMFT

Disclosures

The material in this book is intended to be only informational and not for the purpose of providing mental health or legal advice.

Table of Contents

Trouble Deciding to Stay or Go?.. 9

What You Should Know about Divorce 21

Mine, Yours, Ours: Dividing Things Up 33

I Need Someone to Talk To! 45

What about My Family and Friends? 57

Divorce Happens to the Kids, Too 67

Divorce Is a Loss You Grieve 79

You Are Both Still Their Parents. 91

Financial Issues Are Critical in Divorce................................... 103

When You Want to Start Dating. 113

There Really is Life after Divorce! 125

Six-Word Lessons on Surviving Divorce

Trouble Deciding to Stay or Go?

Everyone's telling me what to do.

You'll hear enough advice to make your head swim: good news stories, dire warnings and people telling you "exactly" what you should do. To avoid hearing advice, say "I'd really rather not talk about it. I'm sure you understand."

You may keep changing your mind.

Getting divorced is a process that involves your whole life--your emotions, finances, day-to-day responsibilities and relationships with everyone. Given all that, expect to waver--often from day to day--at least for a while.

Only you can decide for yourself.

In the last analysis, you are making a choice that only you two can make. Of course, the decision will have an impact on the people you care about the most, but this is your life, after all.

Even when it's obvious, deciding sucks.

You may know in your heart of hearts that splitting up is right for you. That doesn't mean you won't have second thoughts, sleepless nights and high anxiety. These are all normal reactions to a complex situation.

5

But I don't want a divorce.

If you feel you're being forced into divorce or have just been left "high and dry," see both a lawyer and a counselor! The first so you know what options you have, the second to help you work through your feelings.

This can't be happening to us.

At times, the changes in your life may seem unreal, almost like watching someone else's life. That can be a little scary. Just naming how you feel sometimes can help you feel more grounded and safer.

What will everyone say about me?

Ending a marriage involves changing our identity – who we are, how we think about ourselves and believe other people see us. You can't read minds, so don't assume you know what other people think.

I swore I'd never get divorced.

Few people start their marriages thinking they'll divorce. Becoming increasingly unhappy isn't something they want or plan. Relationships sometimes can't be fixed despite efforts to make it work. Acknowledge sadness and loss instead of beating yourself up.

Having an affair betrays our vows.

Affairs can be devastating, of course, but don't automatically assume the marriage is over. A counselor may help you get past your hurt, angry and resentful feelings and find a way to revive your commitment to each other.

Not until the children are grown.

What's the quality of life in your home likely to be? If you and your spouse can avoid constant fighting, staying together could work. Remember, though, a home with chronic conflict is not a healthy place for kids.

Six-Word Lessons on Surviving Divorce

Six-Word Lessons on Surviving Divorce

What You Should Know about Divorce

You need to learn a lot!

Divorce is a legal matter as well as an emotional one. You should understand your options by reading, looking on the internet, talking with people who have gone through it and finding the right advisors.

Take advice to find good advisors.

Ask people you trust what lawyer they'd suggest. Personal recommendations can be very helpful in finding the right person. If you already have a lawyer who doesn't specialize in divorce, ask for a referral to one who does.

Duking it out can get expensive.

The longer the negotiations, the more the divorce is going to cost. Sometimes you can end up fighting just to vent your anger. This is a business negotiation, not an emotional battleground. Try to focus on what really counts.

Get familiar with state divorce laws.

Understanding the law where you live can help you have more realistic expectations about parental rights and the division of property. You'll find lots of information online, in the library and, of course, divorce lawyers can educate you as well.

You get charged for every call.

Lawyers usually charge by the time spent, including phone calls, drafting documents, going to court, etc. They might estimate the likely cost, but, as a rule, the final fees depend on the number of billable hours.

Want to win or be done?

A "good" divorce is one in which both parties feel like they've lost on some issues and won on others. Fighting to win on every issue just to win is very expensive, emotionally and financially **and** delays finalizing the divorce.

What's the lawyer's style and approach?

Request a consultation. Ask about style, attitude toward the other side, accessibilty and references. You need to feel comfortable that your lawyer and you agree about how the process should go.

Who should negotiate the divorce agreement?

When you have kids, a divorce agreement deals with two issues: shared assets and parenting. Divorce attorneys represent only you, sometimes in a highly adversarial way. A divorce mediator is neutral, helping the divorcing couple negotiate many issues themselves.

Could mediation be best for us?

Mediation can be very effective in defusing the emotionality of divorce and can be less expensive. Look for someone who specializes in divorce mediation. Ask lots of questions about the process to see if this approach would work for you.

Should I tell people at work?

The workplace can be a "safe zone" where you don't have to talk or even think about divorce. Telling colleagues on a "need to know" basis might be better than sharing details about your personal situation with all your colleagues.

Six-Word Lessons on Surviving Divorce

Mine, Yours, Ours: Dividing Things Up

Agreeing to a process can help.

Thinking of hiding stuff and hoping you won't get caught? Taking whatever you want without talking about it? Not good plans. You should discuss the guidelines you both will follow before you start divvying up your things.

What's mine is mine, isn't it?

Only when it's clear who "owns what." Be sure to label things clearly so there's no confusion later on. There could be some disagreement about ownership of more items than you expect.

Taking turns isn't only for playgrounds.

For those items you both want, taking turns works well and can help build a cooperative post-divorce relationship. Try flipping a coin to decide who goes first. Perhaps you'll need to trade one item for another you both want.

CDs are yours, everything else – MINE!

Even if you didn't learn to share in nursery school, you need to recognize that you are dividing a home that you both built and care about. Don't take out your hurt and resentment in the dividing-up process.

I should keep all the jewelry.

This is usually a very sensitive issue. Check with your lawyer to clarify what items are legally yours. Family heirlooms are especially complicated. Should those items be returned or could you both agree to put them aside for your children?

I'm not giving in this time!

When you're emotionally so raw, everything can become a battleground. Think about the practical and sentimental value you attach to specific items. Let go of the ones you want just because your soon-to-be ex wants them.

My life shouldn't change that much.

Whatever agreements you both reach, your life will certainly change a lot. Difficult though change is, now is an opportunity to make choices about some things you want to be different You may have options you didn't have before.

I'm the victim.
I get everything.

You may feel you are the injured party and therefore entitled to anything you want. The reality is that you both may have rights to your joint property.

This just won't feel like home.

Of course, the home you're accustomed to will change, even if you stay in the same space. Remind yourself that home is about the relationships between the people living there. What can you do to create or recreate a home?

I don't really care about possessions.

You may feel that way now. However, someday you may regret not having some objects that are meaningful to you and your kids. Divide up what you bought together. Wait a while before deciding what to get rid of.

Six-Word Lessons on Surviving Divorce

I Need Someone to Talk To!

Expect strong, confusing and difficult emotions.

Deciding to divorce, getting a divorce and dealing with being single again are highly emotional experiences. You may feel angry, anxious, disoriented or depressed, often all at once.

Judging when you need professional help

If you're finding your mood disrupts your work and home routines continually, ask an objective and well-trained professional how you're doing. If you are thinking about hurting yourself or someone else, get help immediately!

Psychiatrists and counselors: what's the difference?

Psychiatrists are physicians who specialize in treating mood disorders, like depression and anxiety. They can prescribe medication. Professionals you talk to about problems including psychologists, social workers, life coaches, counselors and therapists aren't physicians and don't prescribe medication.

What should I expect in therapy?

You should feel a solid connection with your therapist. Evaluate whether you've hit it off and you feel comfortable talking honestly about your situation Therapy is about *you,* not the therapist.

How will I react to meds?

As with any medication, you need to be educated about possible side effects, what you can expect to feel and when. Always follow doctor's orders when taking any medication.

No time to see a profesional?

While you may need to do some juggling, making time to talk to a professional when you need it should be a priority at this very difficult time. You can't take care of anyone else if you're falling apart.

Getting therapy makes me look weak.

Think of therapy as you do any other kind of professional help. Getting what you need is much more important than worrying about how it might look. Remember counseling is confidential.

So I'm drinking a little more.

How much more? How often? Alone? In the morning? Until you black out? Got a DUI? Don't use your friends' drinking habits as a guide. If you are or someone else who knows you is worried, consult a professional.

Will I always feel this awful?

No. Dealing with divorce is a process. Like with all grieving, you might feel confused, angry, hurt, relieved, abandoned, sad and almost any other feeling you can name. Over time, you'll reach a new normal.

Do the kids need professional help?

Divorce stresses kids out. A counselor who knows the kids and the situation can evaluate what's happening, reassure you, recommend interventions when needed, and provide objective advice to you and your ex, especially when you disagree.

Six-Word Lessons on Surviving Divorce

What about My Family and Friends?

Am I divorcing my inlaws, too?

Not necessarily but perhaps. Often families think they need to take one side against the other. Making an explicit statement about wanting to continue to be connected is a good first step.

I know they'll all blame me.

Others may blame one of you or the other. Remind them (and yourself) that it usually takes two to make a marriage work and not work. Take the initiative to stay in touch with the people you care about.

They'll always be the kids' grandparents.

Absolutely! Your kids need all the loving family they can get. Maintaining a good relationship for the kids' sake may be difficult initially, but may be easier over time.

No, thanks, you can't fix this.

People who care about you are likely to offer lots of suggestions, sometime with great conviction. Remember, you don't have to "obey" advice. Listening is fine, but you're the one who has to work through the issues.

I need your support right now.

Be direct about how important caring and encouragement are to you especially when you're feeling vulnerable, scared and perhaps overwhelmed. Say it! Be sure to say "thank you," too.

Other people may be upset, too.

You can expect people who care about you to be very worried and distressed about what's happening. Tell them you appreciate their concern, but, remember, it's not your job to convince them about anything. This is your life.

47

I want to tell the world!

You may want to convince other people that the divorce isn't your fault by sharing all the unpleasant details However, constantly bad mouthing your ex could push people away just when you want their compassion and support.

I'm afraid I'll lose my friends.

Friends might feel they need to choose sides. Tell your friends that you understand they may struggle with being loyal to only one of you. Let them know how much you value their friendship and don't want to lose them.

We need to stay with you.

Divorce has financial consquences. You may need to move in with family or friends. Be sure you understand and respect the house rules. Recognize that you're in someone else's home, even if it's family. Act like a **very** polite guest.

Divorce Happens to the Kids, Too

Don't put kids in the middle!

You and your ex need to talk directly to one another even if it's tough. Research tells us making your kids choose sides is the unhealthiest part of divorce for kids!

You're more strict here than there.

It's not a popularity contest! You'll probably have different rules than your ex does. Remember, you're in charge in your home. Kids understand that fact, even though they may push you to be more lenient by comparing you to your ex.

I don't like living with you.

Kids very quickly recognize what buttons to push to get what they want. Threatening to move out can be one way to pressure you. Where they live is up to you and your ex, not to them.

I'm not a grownup, you know.

Sometimes, one child or another seems to take on the responsibilities of the parent who has moved out. Kids shouldn't be your confidant, friend or a substitute adult. Doing chores is fine, but remember to let them be kids.

Get back together again, please, please!

Children often have fantasies about their parents' reconciling. They readily pick up on the ambivalent feelings one or both parents have. Accept their feelings but don't mislead them. Help them understand that the divorce is permanent.

Why can't you stay married anyhow?

Children shouldn't know all the reasons for your divorce. Tell them, "We weren't able to make each other happy, even though we tried. This isn't your fault We're both still your parents and we'll take good care of you."

Will I get to see grandma?

The kids are not divorcing your inlaws. Making sure children know they are not losing their extended family, too, can help recreate stability in their world.

I don't need either of you.

Kids do need their parents, even though they might insist they don't. Keep reminding them that you are there for them, although you're living in different places. And be sure you really are there for them!

I'm not talking to you anymore.

Refusing to communicate may mean your children are feeling overwhelmed. Naming and accepting their hurt, anger, fear, disappointment and other difficult emotions help children feel it's safe to talk about what's happening to them.

Usual behavior or a serious problem?

Changes in what is normal behavior (sleep, grades and behavior in school, expressions of anger, breaking rules) can just be part of growing up. When patterns emerge or the behavior seems really extreme, consult a professional.

Six-Word Lessons on Surviving Divorce

Divorce Is a Loss You Grieve

What are the steps in grieving?

Therese Rando, a bereavement expert, says we go through six stages after a loss:

1. Recognition
2. Reaction
3. Remembering
4. Letting go
5. Readjusting
6. Moving on

Understanding and accepting that you're grieving helps you reach a new normal.

I thought I was doing okay.

Feelings can sneak up on you, even when you think you're over the hard part. Being distressed again doesn't mean you're not dealing with your feelings, just that loss is hard. If you're continually overwhelmed, see a professional.

Sad? I'm just furious every day.

Anger can distract you from fears about the future, feeling lonely and unlovable and other emotions that are difficult to tolerate. If you're consumed by a rage you can't control, a professional could help you understand and manage your feelings.

But I was never getting divorced.

People don't plan to divorce when they marry but it happens. Getting a divorce is the loss of the dreams we had about "forever" and a certain kind of life. Finding new dreams is part of recovering from divorce.

Our life wasn't worse than theirs.

Sometimes what other couples tolerate gives us perspective about our own situation. However, the decision to divorce is entirely personal. Whatever other people do can't determine what's best for you and your family.

I feel like such a failure.

Thinking of yourself as a failure is natural *and* counterproductive. Understanding what contribution you made to the difficulties in your relationship can help you grow, know yourself better and help you approach a new relationship with more wisdom.

Everyone tells me to shape up.

There's no right way or time frame for getting over losses. If you're not functioning, consumed with anger and obsessed about the divorce over an extended period of time, find a counselor who can help you assess how you're doing.

Will ever I feel like myself?

You'll integrate this experience into a different way of living your life. But you'll still be you. Your new "myself" will emerge eventually, probably reflecting that your life has changed in a very profound way.

68

Will I ever trust anyone again?

Learning to trust someone else should build over time, developing confidence in your judgment, having shared experiences, then believing in someone else. "Trust but verify" is a good motto. Take enough time to understand yourself and the other person.

My dreams won't ever come true.

You've lost the dream of "forever" in your relationship. Part of the healing process is about shaping new dreams for yourself. What would you like to do differently? What have you been reluctant to try out? Explore new possibilities?

You Are Both Still Their Parents

How should we tell the kids?

Ideally, you'll agree on what to say and will tell them together. Kids need to hear that they'll be safe, still have two parents who love them and that the divorce isn't their fault. Don't make them choose sides!

I know what's best for kids.

Disagreements over disciplining the children are common when parenting. During a divorce, these disagreements may become more acute. Using the kids as a battleground for the hurt, sadness and anger you quite possibly may experience is extremely destructive to everyone.

Negotiating a parenting agreement is tough.

Co-parenting involves many details, including day-to-day, vacations, holiday schedules, medical care, housing, clothes and afterschool activities to name just a few. A parent coordinator can help you reach an agreement about how the new way of parenting will work.

Of course I know what's best.

You may think only you know what's right. Even so, respecting each other's opinion while having diffferent rules helps the kids avoid being caught in an unhealthy loyalty bind. They'll figure out what's allowed in each place.

Should we follow the agreement exactly?

Sticking firmly to the parenting agreement at first is usually a good idea. Easing up later on may be appropriate. Don't criticize your ex to the kids about breaking the agreement. Don't ask the kids to carry messages about any changes!

Can we ever modify the agreement?

Over time, your kids' needs, interests and priorities may shift. When this happens, it may be time to re-examine the guidelines you agreed to when you were getting a divorce. Ask the kids for input, too, since it's about them.

We need an objective party's input.

Great idea! Think about getting professional help setting up the agreement. A well-drafted agreement can prevent fights over issues that could be resolved amicably. Look for a counselor or mediator experienced in working with divorced couples.

The kids shouldn't make the rules.

Most kids can figure out "how to play the system" and may try to manipulate you by saying what's allowed when they're with the other parent. Say firmly, "These are the rules you need to follow when you're with me."

Why can't we agree on anything?

Finding common ground is tough, especially when emotions are raw and the newness of the arrangement seems overwhelming. Try remembering what you agreed about before. Really listen to what's being said, rather than defending your own position.

Can I really do it myself?

Feeling intimidated is naturally part of the new way you'll be living. Talk to other people who are in the same situation. Look for a group focused on "recovering" from divorce. Remember you were competent before and can be again.

Six-Word Lessons on Surviving Divorce

Financial Issues Are Critical in Divorce

Why should my kids be punished?

Financially, life may well be different. You can help your kids understand that there isn't as much money available as there used to be. Try not to blame your ex to the kids. Don't put them in the middle!

The divorce settlement just isn't fair.

It's not about fair. It's a business negotiation that's difficult to look at objectively. There are too many emotions swirling around. See what the law in your state says to be sure your expectations are realistic.

Talking about money is really crass.

Wrong!. Talking about money is appropriate when ending an economic partnership through divorce. You need to be active in learning about what's going on, even if you haven't before. Read books and ask lots of questions.

I've never had a job before.

Do some research about how others approach job hunting--the internet, books, librarians all can help. Use a skills-based resume that emphasizes what you've learned managing a house and family. Think about getting trained for a new profession.

I won't survive when alimony ends.

Plan, plan, plan. Check out retraining and going back to school. Learn job search skills. Read books. Ask friends and family who you should be talking to. Don't wait until the last check arrives to figure it out!

How should I handle my investments?

Read some books – ones that are written for those new to investing. Talk to friends and family about who they trust. Interview financial planners. Ask questions, lots of them. Take your time to make decisions.

86

I can't even balance a checkbook!

Ask staff at your bank for help. They can show you how to read a statement, write checks and manage your account well. Don't worry about looking foolish. Foolish is not learning what you need to know.

Who decides on the kids' allowances?

Allowances are a way to teach children how to handle money. You and your ex may have different ideas about what's appropriate. Start by writing down what the allowance should pay for – see if you agree.

88

My quality of life is ruined.

Your life may change because your finances are more limited than before. Remember you are more than the things you own. Think carefully about what you really care about--your values. How can you create a values-based life?

When You Want to Start Dating

89

How do I meet other singles?

Feeling lonely and unloved is terribly painful. Having new relationships can be a healthy step toward rebuilding your life. Community activities, cultural offerings, parenting groups are good places to meet new friends who share your interests.

Who decides when I can date?

You do! Your kids, family and friends may have different ideas, but you don't need their permission. You are an adult and entitled to make your own decisions. Be aware that this may be a sensitive issue for other people.

Should my kids meet my *Someone*?

When you're dating someone special fairly regularly, you and that person can talk about "when." If you both feel comfortable together, a casual family outing can be a good setting for introductions.

Will my dating hurt the kids?

Kids often fantasize about their parents getting back together again, so they may be unhappy that you're moving forward in your life. In the long run, kids can learn to accept the "new normal" in their lives.

When should all the kids meet?

That all depends on a number of factors – on the ages of the kids, how they're adjusting to the divorce, how serious the relationship seems to be. If they do meet, try to keep it relaxed and fun!

Will all the kids get along?

Sometimes they will and sometimes they won't. Just like siblings in any family, kids squabble, complain and feel put upon. Don't expect perfect harmony, just as you don't with your own kids. Make clear rules together and stick to them.

95

I don't want to be alone.

Being on your own is tough, but it can be a way to get to know and like yourself better. Be careful about getting involved in another relationship just to avoid being single.

Should a date go with me?

Going to an event or party with a date is a big step for many people, including other people at the party. Be prepared for different reactions from friends and family: some may be supportive while others may disapprove.

The kids must always come first.

Not really. Of course, you take their needs into consideration, but you are entitled to build a new life for yourself, too. Finding the right balance your needs and those of your kids is an ongoing task for all parents.

Am I desperate and just settling?

Making a commitment to a new relationship is complicated. Wanting to be with someone can be very powerful. When you're unsure, slow down. Take time to get to know that other person and to know yourself. Then follow your instincts.

Six-Word Lessons on Surviving Divorce

There Really is Life after Divorce!

# Did I make a terrible mistake?

Having second thoughts about a life-changing decision is quite normal, especially when the reality of how different your life is sinks in. As you reach a new normal, painful "what if's" are likely to subside. Hang in there!

Discovering yourself and your new normal.

Surviving divorce is definitely tough. Your life *will* be different, yet you might prefer living without disappointment, frustration and tension. While challenging and scary, reinventing yourself may give you choices you never had before. Good luck on the journey!

See the entire Six-Word Lesson Series at *6wordlessons.com*

Want to talk about divorce issues?

Contact Barbara at *futurescoach.net*

Read more about Barbara at *futurescoach.net*

www.ingramcontent.com/pod-product-compliance
Lightning Source LLC
Chambersburg PA
CBHW070643050426
42451CB00008B/279